DARE TO DREAM

(VOL 1)

AMIT DEB

BlueRose Publishers
New Delhi • London

First Published in March 2022

ISBN: 978-93-93809-86-5

BLUEROSE PUBLISHERS
www.bluerosepublishers.com
info@bluerosepublishers.com
+91 8882 898 898

Cover Design:
Geetika Kandari

Typographic Design:
Tanya Raj Upadhyay

Distributed by: BlueRose, Amazon, Flipkart

Preface

I have chosen to write this book to share a few struggling stories of sportspersons. They did tremendous hard work to achieve goals in their respective disciplines. While you read their stories, you will feel the pain they took to earn their medals.

The stories which I have mentioned will inspire you to achieve something in your life. It's the mind which controls everything, if we can give a command to our mind that "yes I can" then nothing is impossible in this world. These stories will make you strong mentally, your mind will be determined to attain your goals.

It's the attitude that matters a lot. These stories will inject in your mind a " Never give up attitude".

If they can achieve their goal then why can't we, after all, we are also human beings.

Discipline is the key, we fail in our life because we give up after one failure.

This book will bring a change in your lifestyle and mindset.

Acknowledgment

Walking through life, I have always seen myself as a learner, surrounded by people with a strong mind who have inspired me to achieve goals in my life.

I would like to express my heartfelt gratitude to all who have suggested writing another book.

It will be impossible to name all of them but some of them are my parents, family members, colleagues, VV runners group, my friends.

My special gratitude to Mrs. Paridhi Ojha (sports physiotherapist), Dr. Shailendra Kumar (orthopedic surgeon) who did splendid jobs and kept on pushing me to stay motivated.

Also, special thanks to the team of Divine Arts Lab who has worked tirelessly and supported me throughout this journey.

I owe a million thanks to all those sportspersons who have given their heart and soul to perform at the highest level.

And of course, my warm thanks to the entire team of Blue Rose publishers, their intense efforts and sincere dedication are visible on every page of the book. This journey with them has been about not only working on a book but also bonding deeply with the publisher.

About the author

Amit Deb is a marathoner, cyclist, YouTuber, blogger, and fitness guru.

Holding an engineering degree in Mechanical and a master's in Thermal Power Plants, his recent book " Friendship with Fitness" has done very well, people are appreciating the contents of the book.

This has inspired him to write a book on sportspeople's journeys to achieve their goal.

Now this book is an attempt to share inspirational stories to everyone to change your life.

Emphasizing that Health leads to Happiness And being fit adds more healthy years to life, his mantra is " fitness is life and fitness is everything".

Struggling journey of the author

Let me share my struggling journey, well my full-fledged fitness journey started in 2013. Till July 2019, participated in 30 timed half marathons and many 10km timed events. Everything was going on very well but suddenly during practice, I felt pain in my heel. Initially, I ignored it but gradually the pain was increasing. So, I decided to visit a doctor. After doing MRI, it was revealed that the Achilles tendon has partially ruptured. The doctor advised going for PRP (platelet-rich plasma) therapy. So, in this regard, discussed with so many doctors, everyone suggested the same. After doing PRP therapy, was on aircast shoes for 21 days.

During this period, I was so much frustrated after seeing that all my running partners were participating in Airtel Delhi Half Marathon. When I saw their pics and timings, I cried so badly, and only I could feel that pain. Then I promised myself that " I will come back". After 21 days, removed my aircast shoe and visited Sporting Ethos, South Ex, New Delhi. My coach Mr. Sanjay Dasila apprised me about this center and also introduced me to sports physiotherapist Mrs. Paridhi Ojha.

She began to work on this and the progress was visible. She always used to say that " believe in yourself, one day you will run again". Then after 6 months, started my practice but still, some pain was there. Then I met Dr. Shailendra Kumar, SSB hospital, Faridabad. After seeing my reports, he suggested going for another PRP, so did it again. Then after a few days, the physiotherapy process started. Yes, the result was remarkable but because of the pandemic, my running got halted.

So, bought gym equipment and set up a home gym. Started working on core strength, then after lockdown, started my practice. Recently started participating in running events.

During this painful journey, I have learned that " Never say die and trust the process".

Table of Contents

Derek Anthony Redmond (Athlete)

Derek Anthony Redmond is a retired British sprinter. Redmond was born on 3rd September 1965 in Buckinghamshire to West Indian immigrants and educated at Roade School, Northamptonshire, where a multi-use sports hall is named after him.

During his career, he held the British record for the 400 meters sprint and won gold medals in the 4x400 meters relay at the World Championships and European Championships.

At the 1991 World Championships Redmond was a member of the British team that shocked the athletics world by beating the much-favored American team into second place to claim the gold medal in the 4x400 meters relay. Redmond ran the second leg in the final and, together with teammates Roger Black, John Regis, and Kriss Akabusi ran what was then the second-fastest 4x400 meters relay in history.

<u>**1992 Summer Olympics (inspirational moment):**</u>

Redmond was in good form by the time of the Barcelona Olympics. He posted the fastest time of the first round and went on to win his quarter-final. In the semi-final, Redmond started well, but in the back straight about 250 meters from the finish, his hamstring tore.

He hobbled to a halt and then fell to the ground in pain. Stretcher-bearers made their way over to him, but he wanted to finish the race. He began to hobble along the track. He was soon joined on the track by his father, Jim Redmond, who barged past security and on to the track to get to his son. Jim and Derek completed the lap of the track together, with Derek leaning on his father's shoulder for support.

As they crossed the finish line, the crowd of 65,000 spectators rose to give Derek a standing ovation. However, as his father had helped him finish, Derek was officially disqualified and Olympic records state that he "Did Not Finish" the race.

Redmond's struggle in the 1992 semi-final later became the subject of one of the International Olympic Committee's "Celebrate Humanity" videos, which proclaimed: "Strength is measured in pounds. Speed is measured in seconds. **<u>You can't measure courage</u>**".

In 2008, Redmond was featured in the "Go World" series of Visa Advertisements promoting the Olympic Games. The advertisement highlights his 1992 injury, noting that he and his father finished dead last, but he and his father finished.

<u>**Achievements:**</u>

Sl no	Year	Description
1	1985	Broke the British record for the 400 meters in 1985 with a run of 44.82 seconds.
2	1986	Redmond was a member of the team that won the 4x400 meters relay gold medal Championships.
3	1987	He was on the team that won the 4x400 meters relay silver medal at the World Championships.

Injuries consistently interrupted Redmond's career. At the 1988 Olympics in Seoul, he pulled out of the opening round of the 400 meters 90 seconds before his heat because of an injury to his Achilles tendon. Before the 1992 Summer Olympics, he had undergone eight operations due to injuries.

Two years after the Olympics in Barcelona, he was told by a surgeon that he would never run again or represent his country in sport. However, after coming to terms with the loss of athletics as a career, he began to turn his attention, with the encouragement of his father, to other sports that he enjoyed. He went on to play professional basketball for the Birmingham Bullets.

Redmond currently does motivational speaking on the conference circuit, inspiring people with the story of the 4x400 gold medal triumph and his famous ordeal in the 1992 Barcelona Olympics.

Dave Wottle (Athlete)

Dave Wottle was born in Canton, Ohio. During his childhood, he was very slim and feeble. His family doctor told him that he needed to do something, such as running, to strengthen himself. The young boy took this advice and started to run.

During his college days, he participated in the mile run, he finished second at the 1970 NCAA Outdoor Track and Field Championships.

During the 1971 season, Wottle was hampered by injuries, but a year later in 1972 he won the 1,500-meter race at the NCAA Outdoor Track and Field Championships, and at the 1973 NCAA Outdoor Track and Field Championships he won the mile run in a time of 3:57.1.

Leading up to the 1972 Olympic Games in Munich, Germany, Wottle won the AAU 800-meter title before equalling the world record over 800 meters of 1:44.3 at the US Olympic Trials.

<u>Turning point:</u>

In the 800-meter final at the Olympics, Wottle immediately dropped to the rear of the field and stayed there for the first 500 m, at which point he started to pass runner after runner up the final straightaway.

He seized the lead in the final stretch to beat pre-race favorite Yevgeny Arzhanov of the Soviet Union by just 0.03 seconds. This gained him the nickname of "The Head Waiter". (Another nickname was "Wottle the Throttle").

Stunned by his victory, Wottle forgot to remove his cap on the podium during the national anthem. This was interpreted by some as a form of protest, but Wottle later apologized at the news conference following the medals ceremony.

He also competed in the 1500 meter run at the Munich Olympics, but he was eliminated in the semi-finals.

His signature cap was originally used for practical purposes. He sported long hair at the peak of his career, so the hat kept his hair out of his face. After realizing the cap was part of his identity and for good luck, he wore it for the remainder of his career.

Wottle turned professional in 1974 but retired quite soon after that. Later, he became a college track coach at Walsh College (Ohio) (1975–77) and Bethany College (West Virginia) where he also served as Director of Admissions (1977–81).

Balbir Singh (Hockey)

Balbir Singh (10 October 1924 – 25 May 2020) was an Indian hockey player. Singh was born in Punjab. His father was a freedom fighter who was absent most of Singh's early years due to being frequently jailed.

At the age of twelve, Singh saw a newsreel on India's 1936 Olympic hockey triumph, which sparked his interest in hockey. Singh led the Khalsa college hockey team to three consecutive championships as captain and was soon playing for the Punjab state team. He helped the Punjab state team win two consecutive national titles in 1946 and 1947.

He was a three-time Olympic gold medallist, having played a key role in India's wins in London (1948), Helsinki (1952) (as vice-captain), and Melbourne (1956) (as captain) Olympics.

Achievements in Olympics:

1948 London Olympics:

Singh's first appearance at the 1948 London Olympics was in the match against Argentina. After that, he played in the Final against Great Britain. Singh scored the first two goals and India won by 4–0.

1952 Helsinki Olympics:

Singh was vice-captain of the 1952 Olympic team, with K. D. Singh as the Captain. Balbir was India's flag bearer in the opening ceremony. He scored a hat trick against Britain in the semi-final, which India won 3–1. He scored five goals in India's 6–1 win against the Netherlands setting a new Olympic record for most goals scored by an individual in an Olympic final in men's field hockey.

1956 Melbourne Olympics:

Singh, captain of the 1956 Olympic team, scored five goals in the opening match against Afghanistan but was then injured. **Randhir Singh Gentle** captained the rest of the group matches. Singh had to skip the group matches but played in the semi-final and the final. India won the final match against Pakistan with a result of 1–0.

In a total of 8 Olympic matches he played, he scored 22 goals for his nation.

Inspiration:

He is regarded as one of the greatest hockey players of all time and is widely regarded as the sport's greatest ever center-forward.

Singh was the manager and chief coach of the Indian team for the 1975 Men's Hockey World Cup, which India won, and the 1971 Men's Hockey World Cup, where India earned a bronze medal.

During the London Olympics in 2012, Singh was honored in the Olympic Museum exhibition, *"The*

Olympic Journey: The Story of the Games," held at the Royal Opera House.

The exhibition told the story of the Olympic Games from its creation in 776BC through to the London 2012 Olympic Games. He was one of the 16 iconic Olympians recognized as an example "of human strength and endeavor, of passion, determination, hard work, and achievement and demonstrates the values of the Olympic Movement".

Awards:

Sl no	Year	Description
1	1957	Padma Shri.
2	1977	He wrote an autobiography "The Golden Hat Trick".
3	2006	He was named the Best Sikh Hockey Player.
4	2008	He wrote the book "The Golden Yardstick".
5	2015	He was conferred with the Major Dhyan Chand Lifetime Achievement Award of Hockey India.
6	2021	The Mohali International Hockey Stadium has been renamed the Olympian Balbir Singh Senior International Hockey Stadium in honor of his death anniversary.

Sandeep Singh (Hockey)

Sandeep Singh (born 27 February 1986) is an Indian professional field hockey player from Haryana and an ex-captain of the Indian national hockey team. He generally features as a penalty corner specialist for the team. He has been dubbed "Flicker Singh" in the media for his specialization of the drag-flick, one of the fastest in the world.

Career highlights:

Sandeep's international debut was in January 2004 in Sultan Azlan Shah Cup in Kuala Lumpur. He took over as the captain of the Indian national team in January 2009, and Rajpal Singh succeeded him later in 2010.

His drag-flick speed of 145 km/h has been one of the best in the world.

Under his captaincy, the Indian team managed to clinch the Sultan Azlan Shah Cup in 2009 after defeating Malaysia in the finals at Ipoh. India won the title after a long wait of 13 years. Singh was also the top goal scorer of the Sultan Azlan Shah Cup tournament.

The team had a resounding victory over France in the finals of the Olympic qualifiers (2012) by beating France 9–1. Ace drag-flicker Singh starred in the final against France by scoring five goals – including a hat-trick – all from penalty corners (19th, 26th, 38th, 49th, and 51st minutes). Singh was the highest scorer of the Olympic qualifiers tournament by scoring 16 goals.

<u>Turning point</u>:

On 22 August 2006, Singh was seriously injured after being hit by an accidental gunshot in the *Kalka Shatabdi Express* train, while on his way to join the national team due to leave for the World Cup in Africa two days later.

He was almost paralyzed and in a wheelchair for 1 year of his life. He was 20 at that time.

Singh not only recovered from that serious injury but also established himself again and played the world cup for India in the 2010 Indian team.

<u>Achievements</u>:

Sl no	Year	Description
1	2004	Junior Asia Cup top scorer.
2	2008	Top scorer in Sultan Azlan Shah cup.
3	2009	Top scorer in Sultan Azlan Shah Cup, a man of the tournament.
4	2010	Asian Games top scorer, Arjuna awardee.
5	2013	Top scorer in Hockey India League.
6	2014	Top scorer in Hockey India League.
7	2018	Indian filmmaker Shaad Ali made a biographical film, titled *Soorma* (lit. 'Warrior'), based on Singh's life. Diljit Dosanjh played Sandeep Singh's role in the film.

Jesse Owens (Athlete)

James Cleveland "Jesse" Owens (September 12, 1913 – March 31, 1980) was an American track and field athlete who won four gold medals at the 1936 Olympic Games.

Jesse Owens, originally known as *J.C.*, was born on September 12, 1913.

As a youth, Owens took different menial jobs in his spare time: he delivered groceries, loaded freight cars, and worked in a shoe repair shop while his father and older brother worked at a steel mill. During this period, Owens realized that he had a passion for running. Throughout his life, Owens attributed the success of his athletic career to the encouragement of Charles

Riley, his junior high school track coach at Fairmount Junior High School. Since Owens worked in a shoe repair shop after school, Riley allowed him to practice before school instead.

Owens first came to national attention when he was a student of East Technical High School in Cleveland; he equaled the world record of 9.4 seconds in the 100 yards (91 m) dash and long-jumped 24 feet 9+½ inches (7.56 m) at the 1933 National High School Championship in Chicago.

Owens specialized in the sprints and the long jump and was recognized in his lifetime as "perhaps the greatest and most famous athlete in track and field history". He set three world records and tied another, all in less than an hour, at the 1935 Big Ten track meet in Ann Arbor, Michigan—a feat that has never been equaled and has been called "the greatest 45 minutes ever in sport".

<u>Achievements in 1936 summer Olympics:</u>

- On August 3, Owens won the 100 m dash with a time of 10.3 seconds, defeating a teammate and a college friend **Ralph Metcalfe** by a tenth of a second and defeating **Tinus Osendarp** of the Netherlands by two-tenths of a second.

- On August 4, he won the long jump with a leap of 8.06 meters (26 ft 5 in) (3¼ inches short of his world record). He later credited this achievement to the technical advice that he received from **Luz Long,** the German competitor whom he defeated.

- On August 5, he won the 200 m sprint with a time of 20.7 seconds, defeating teammate **Mack Robinson** (the older brother of **Jackie Robinson**).

- On August 9, Owens won his fourth gold medal in the 4 × 100 m sprint relay. Owens's record-breaking performance of four gold medals was not equaled until **Carl Lewis** won gold medals in the same events at the **1984 Summer Olympics** in **Los Angeles**.

The Jesse Owens Award is USA Track and Field's highest accolade for the year's best track and field athlete. Owens was ranked by ESPN as the sixth greatest North American athlete of the 20th century and the highest-ranked in his sport. In 1999, he was on the six-man shortlist for the BBC's Sports Personality of the Century.

Founder of **Adidas** athletic shoe company **Adi Dassler** visited Owens in the Olympic village and persuaded Owens to wear Gebrüder Dassler Schuhfabrik shoes; this was the first sponsorship for a male African American athlete.

Owens had set the world record in the long jump with a leap of 8.13 m (26 ft 8 in) in 1935, the year before the Berlin Olympics, and this record stood for 25 years until it was broken in 1960 by countryman **Ralph Boston**.

<u>Owens was quoted saying the secret behind his success was, "I let my feet spend as little time on the ground as possible. From the air, fast down, and from the ground, fast up</u>."

After the games had ended, the entire Olympic team was invited to compete in **Sweden**. Owens decided to capitalize on his success by returning to the United States to take up some of the more lucrative endorsement offers. United States athletic officials were furious and withdrew his amateur status, which immediately ended his career. Owens was angry and stated that "A fellow desires something for himself."

Owens argued that the **racial discrimination** he had faced throughout his athletic career, such as not being eligible for scholarships in college and therefore being unable to take classes between training and working to pay his way, meant he had to give up on amateur athletics in pursuit of financial gain elsewhere.

Owens returned home from the 1936 Olympics with four gold medals and international fame, yet had difficulty finding work. He took on menial jobs as a gas station attendant, playground janitor, and manager of a dry-cleaning firm.

Owens was prohibited from making appearances at amateur sporting events to bolster his profile, and he found out that the commercial offers had all but disappeared. In 1937, he briefly toured with a twelve-piece jazz band under contract with Consolidated Artists but found it unfulfilling. He also made appearances at baseball games and other events.

Finally, **Willis Ward**—a friend and former competitor from the **University of Michigan**—brought Owens to **Detroit** in 1942 to work at **Ford Motor Company** as Assistant Personnel Director. Owens later became a director, in which capacity he worked until 1946.

He died because of lung cancer at the age of 66 in **Tucson, Arizona**, on March 31, 1980.

<u>Awards & Achievements</u>:

Sl no	Year	Description
1	1936	Athlete of the year.
2	1970	**Alabama Sports Hall of Fame.**
3	1976	Awarded **Presidential Medal of Freedom** by President **Gerald Ford.**

4	1979	Awarded **Living Legend Award** by President **Jimmy Carter.**
5	1981	**USA Track and Field** created the **Jesse Owens Award** which is given annually to the country's top track and field athlete.
6	1990	Awarded the **Congressional Gold Medal** by President **George H. W. Bush.**
7	1999	Shortlisted for the BBC's **Sports Personality of the Century.**
8	2001	**Ohio State University** dedicated **Jesse Owens Memorial Stadium** for track and field events.
9	2009	**World Athletic Championships** in Berlin, all members of the United States Track and Field team wore badges with "JO" on them to commemorate Owens's victories in the same stadium 73 years before.
10	2010	**Ohio Historical Society** proposed Owens as a finalist from a statewide vote for inclusion in **Statuary Hall** at the **United States Capitol.**
11	2018	Ohio Governor **John Kasich** dedicated the 75th state park Jesse Owens, State Park.

Literature and film

- 1984: An **Emmy Award**-winning biographical **television film** of Owens's life, *The Jesse Owens Story*, is released, with **Dorian Harewood** portraying Owens.

- 2006: *The Book Thief* by **Markus Zusak** is released, in which a character named Rudy Steiner idolizes Owens.

- 2016: A feature film titled *Race* about Owens with **Stephan James** portraying Owens was released.

Ted Williams (Baseball)

Theodore Samuel Williams (August 30, 1918 – July 5, 2002) was an American professional baseball player and manager. He played his entire 19-year Major League Baseball (MLB) career, primarily as a left fielder for the Boston Red Sox from 1939 to 1960.

His career was interrupted by military service during World War II and the Korean War. Nicknamed "**Teddy Ballgame**", "**The Kid**", "**The Splendid Splinter**", and "**The Thumper**", Williams is regarded as one of the greatest hitters in baseball history.

Williams was born and raised in San Diego. At the age of 8, he was taught how to throw a baseball by his uncle, Saul Venzor. As a child, Williams's heroes were Pepper Martin of the St. Louis Cardinals and Bill Terry of the New York Giants. Williams graduated from Herbert Hoover High School in San Diego, where he played baseball as a pitcher and was the star of the team.

During this time, he also played American Legion Baseball, later being named the 1960 American Legion Baseball Graduate of the Year.

Williams played baseball throughout his youth. After joining the Red Sox in 1939, he immediately emerged as one of the sport's best hitters.

Williams was required to interrupt his baseball career in 1943 to serve three years in the United States Navy and Marine Corps during World War II. Upon returning to MLB in 1946, Williams won his first AL MVP Award and played in his only World Series.

In 1947, he won his second Triple Crown. Williams was returned to active military duty for portions of the 1952 and 1953 seasons to serve as a Marine combat aviator in the Korean War.

In 1957 and 1958 at the ages of 39 and 40, respectively, he was the AL batting champion for the fifth and sixth time.

He was selected for the Major League Baseball All-Time Team in 1997 and the Major League Baseball All-Century Team in 1999.

Playing style:

Williams was an obsessive student of hitting. He famously used a lighter bat than most sluggers, because it generated a faster swing. In 1970 he wrote a book on the subject, *The Science of Hitting* (revised 1986), which is still read by many baseball players. The book describes his theory of swinging only at pitches that came into ideal areas of his strike zone, a strategy Williams credited with his success as a hitter.

In his last years, Williams suffered from cardiomyopathy. He had a pacemaker implanted in November 2000 and he underwent open-heart surgery in January 2001. After suffering a series of strokes, he died of cardiac arrest at the age of 83 on July 5, 2002.

About his greatness:

In his induction speech, Williams included a statement calling for the recognition of the great Negro leagues players: "I've been a very lucky guy to have worn a baseball uniform, and I hope someday the names of Satchel Paige and Josh Gibson in some way can be added as a symbol of the great Negro players who are not here only because they weren't given a chance."

Williams was referring to two of the most famous names in the Negro leagues, who were not allowed to play because of the color barrier. Gibson died early in 1947 and thus never played in the majors, and Paige's brief major league stint came long past his prime as a player.

This powerful and unprecedented statement from the Hall of Fame podium was "A first crack in the door that ultimately would open and include Paige and Gibson and other Negro League stars in the shrine." Paige was the first inducted in 1971 and it continued on and off into the 21st century.

Awards and recognition:

Sl no	Year	Description
1	1996	Baseball Hall of Fame.
2	1991	President George H. W. Bush presented Williams with the Presidential Medal of Freedom, the highest civilian award in the US.
3	2013	The Bob Feller Act of Valour Award honored Williams as one of 37 Baseball Hall of Fame members for his service in the United States Marine Corps during World War II.

Mihir Sen (Swimmer)

Mihir Sen (16 November 1930 – 11 June 1997) was a famous Indian long-distance swimmer and lawyer.

Mihir Sen was born on 16 November 1930 in Purulia, West Bengal.

Mihir graduated with a degree in law from the Utkal University in Bhubaneswar in Odisha. He wanted to travel to England to prepare himself for the bar but was constrained by a lack of funds.

However, with the financial help of then Chief Minister of Orissa, Biju Patnaik in 1950 he was able to board a ship to England to pursue his studies.

He was the first Asian to conquer the English Channel from Dover to Calais in 1958 and did so in the fourth-fastest time (14 hrs & 45 mins).

He was the only man to swim the oceans of the five continents in one calendar year (1966). These included

- Palk Strait

- Dardanelles

- Bosphorus

- Gibraltar

- Entire length of the Panama Canal

This unique achievement earned him a place in The Guinness Book of Records as the "world's greatest long-distance swimmer".

While he was reading an article in a local newspaper about Florence Chadwick, the first American woman to swim the English Channel in 1950, he was motivated and promised himself to repeat this feat for his country.

But he had hardly any experience in swimming, so he started training to achieve this feat.

On Sept 27, 1958, he crossed the English Channel from Dover to Calais in the fourth-fastest time (14 hours and 45 minutes). He became a National Hero and was considered to be one of the most prominent youth icons of his generation.

In 1959, he was awarded the Padma Shri by Prime Minister Jawaharlal Nehru.

Initially, he needed to raise Rs 45,000 to pay the Indian Navy to record and navigate the Palk Strait swim. Sen raised half the money through sponsors (notably the Kolkata daily, *The Statesman*) and the balance was provided by then Prime Minister Indira Gandhi. She further extended full support of the Indian Navy (The INS Sukanya and the INS Sharada) to accompany him for the Palk Strait swim.

<u>Sen's record timings are</u>:

Sl no	Description	Timing
1	Ceylon (Sri Lanka) and Dhanushkodi (India).	25 hours and 36 minutes
2	Straits of Gibraltar.	08 hours and 01 minute
3	40-mile-long Dardanelles (Gallipoli, Europe to Sedulbahir, Asia minor).	13 hours and 55 minutes
4	(50-mile length) of the Panama Canal.	34 hours and 15 minutes

All these achievements earned him a place in the **<u>Guinness Book of World Records</u>** for long-distance swimming and he was awarded the Padma Bhushan in 1967 by Prime Minister Indira Gandhi.

In the same year, he also won the Blitz Nehru Trophy for 'daring achievements in the seven seas of the world.'

After his return to India in 1958 (shortly after his English Channel victory), he was denied entry into the clubs due to their "whites only" policy. This compelled him to lead a high-profile media campaign to abolish this rule, and, as a result, clubs throughout India were forced to open their doors to all Indians.

Sen died from a combination of Alzheimer's and Parkinson's disease at age 66 in June 1997.

K.D.Jadhav (Wrestler)

Khashaba Dadasaheb Jadhav (January 15, 1926 – August 14, 1984) was an Indian wrestler. He was the first athlete from independent India to win an individual medal in the Olympics.

Born in a village called Goleshwar in Karad taluka of District Satara in Maharashtra State, KD Jadhav was the youngest of five sons of a renowned wrestler Dadasaheb Jadhav.

He grew up in a household that lived and breathed wrestling. He participated in the Quit India Movement providing shelter and a hiding place to the revolutionaries, circulating letters against the British were some of his contributions to the movement.

His father Dadasaheb was a wrestling coach and he initiated Jadhav into wrestling at the age of five.

He resolved to unfurl the tricolor flag in Olympics on Independence Day August 15, 1947

After Norman Pritchard who won two silver medals in athletics in 1900 under colonial India, Jadhav was the first individual athlete from independent India to win a medal at the Olympics.

He is the only Indian Olympic medalist who never received a Padma Award. Jadhav was extremely nimble on his feet, which made him different from other wrestlers of his time.

<u>**Glimpses of Olympics**</u>:

1948 Summer Olympics:

Jadhav's first feel of the big stage was at the 1948 London Olympics; his journey was funded by the Maharaja of Kolhapur. During his stay in London, he was trained by Rees Gardner, a former lightweight world champion from the United States. It was Gardner's guidance that saw Jadhav finish sixth in the flyweight section, despite being unfamiliar with wrestling on the mat.

He stunned the audience by defeating the Australian wrestler Bert Harris in the first few minutes of the bout.

1952 Summer Olympics:

After the marathon bout, he was asked to fight Soviet Union's Rashid Mammadbeyov. As per the rest of the rules of at least 30 minutes were required between bouts, but no Indian official was available to press his case, a tired Jadhav, failed to inspire and Mammadbeyov cashed in on the chance to reach the final.

Defeating the wrestlers from Canada, Mexico, and Germany, he won the bronze medal on 23 July 1952 thereby creating history by becoming Independent India's first individual medal winner.

For years, he was neglected by the sports federation and had to live the final stages of his life in poverty. He died in a road accident in 1984, his wife struggled to get any assistance from any quarter.

Awards and honors:

- He was honored by making him a part of the torch run at the <u>1982 Asian Games</u> in Delhi

- The Maharashtra Government awarded the Chhatrapati Puraskar posthumously in 1992-1993.

- He was posthumously honored with the Arjuna Award in 2001.

- The newly built wrestling venue for the 2010 Delhi Commonwealth Games was named after him to honor his achievements.

Arati Saha (Swimmer)

Arati Saha (24 September 1940 – 23 August 1994) was an Indian long-distance swimmer, best known for becoming the first Asian woman to swim across the English Channel on 29 September 1959.

At the age of four, she would accompany her uncle to the Champatala Ghat bath, where she learned to swim. In 1946, at the age of five, she won the gold medal in 110 yards freestyle at the Shailendra Memorial Swimming Competition, beginning her swimming career.

Her talent was spotted by Sachin Nag, and later she was inspired by the Indian swimmer Mihir Sen to try to cross the English Channel.

<u>**Career**</u>:

Sl no	Year	Description
1	1945-51	Won 22 state-level competitions in West Bengal.
2	1948	She won silver in 100 meters freestyle and 200 meters breaststroke and won bronze in 200 meters freestyle in the national championship.
3	1950	All India record.
4	1951	West Bengal state meet, she clocked 1 minute 37.6 seconds in 100 meters breaststroke and broke Dolly Nazir's all-India record.

| 5 | 1952 Olympics | She represented India at the 1952 Summer Olympics along with compatriot Dolly Nazir. She was one of the four women participants and the youngest member of the Indian contingent at the age of 12. |

Crossing the English Channel:

Arati got the first inspiration to cross the English Channel Channel from Brojen Das, who became the first person from the Indian subcontinent to cross the English Channel.

Greta Andersen, a Danish-born female swimmer from the United States clocked 11 hours and 1 minute and stood first among both men and women. She proposed the name of Arati to the organizers of the Butlin International Cross Channel Swimming Race for the next year's event.

Dr. Arun Gupta, the assistant executive secretary of Hatkhola Swimming Club took the initiative in organizing Arati's participation at the event. He organized exhibits of Arati's swimming prowess as part of a fund-raising program.

While the logistics of her trip were being arranged by govt, Arati began swimming for long hours. On 13 April 1959, Arati swam continuously for eight hours at the pond in Deshbandhu Park.

A total of 58 participants including five women from 23 countries took part in the competition. The race was scheduled for 27 August 1959 at 1 am local time from Cape Gris Nez, France to Sandgate, England. However, the pilot boat of Arati Saha did not arrive in time. By 11 am, she had swum more than 40 miles and came within 5 miles of the England coast. At that point, she faced a current from the opposite direction. As a result, by 4 pm, she could only swim about two more miles, before she had to quit.

Arati prepared herself for a second attempt. Her manager Dr. Arun Gupta was ill, but she carried on with her practice. On 29 September 1959, she made her second attempt. Starting from Cape Gris Nez, France, she swam for 16 hours and 20 minutes, battling tough waves and covered 42 miles to reach Sandgate, England. On reaching the coast of England, she hoisted the Indian flag. Vijaylakshmi Pandit was the first to congratulate her.

Jawahar Lal Nehru and many eminent people personally congratulated her. On 30 September, the All-India Radio announced the achievement of Arati Saha.

She died as a result of an illness on 23rd August 1994.

Awards:

Sl no	Year	Description
1	1960	Padma Shri.
2	1999	Department of Posts introduced a postage stamp of her which was ₹ 3 denomination.
3	2020	She was featured as a Google Doodle.

Bhawana Jat (Race walking)

Her father had only two bighas of land in their village. There was a time when they used to eat just one meal a day because the amount they produced on the farm was less.

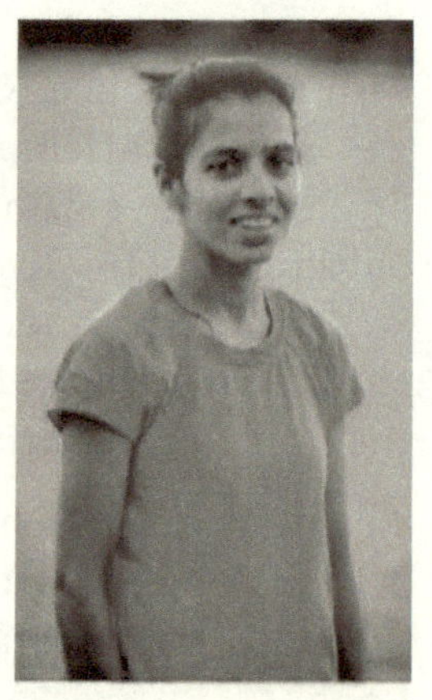

They all lived in a mud hut and she used to train in a small makeshift field near her house at night so that the village elders wouldn't come to know. She used to train barefoot then.

The 24-year-old, hailing from the small village of Kabra in Rajasthan's Rajsamand district, became India's first female race walker to qualify for the Tokyo 2020 Olympics.

She smashed the national record with a timing of 1:29.54 at the 2019 National Open Race-Walking Championship in Ranchi (the Olympic qualification mark was set at 1:31.00). She finished seventh in Rio.

Jat achieved this feat despite never being selected for a senior national or international camp, which is why her competition was caught by surprise. Less than a decade ago, she and her family struggled to even get two meals a day.

Apart from the financial problems, Jat also had to manoeuvre past several societal hurdles - including misogyny - before securing her job at Railways. After seeing her train in shorts, the village panchayat barred her from practicing on the mud field near her house.

Villagers didn't like wearing shorts and practicing, also the actions made by race walkers seemed quite shameful to them. That is why they asked her to stop practicing and asked her to focus on household chores. But her father and brother had immense faith in her talent and made sure that she found certain time slots to practice when people weren't around.

She used to practice at 3 am, before the village woke up, under the watchful eyes of her brother.

During her sub-junior days, her father used to earn around Rs. 2000 a month. That meant she had to borrow spare shoes from competitors to participate in tournaments.

Jat works without pay for Railways right now, having decided to dedicate all her time to training.

She had to repay around Rs. 2 lakh in loans to private money lenders in her district, as she had taken them as expenses for her training, diet, and competition travel. She took a loan to perform better in the Tokyo Olympics and thought that if she can win a medal there, then definitely she will be able to pay it back with the required interest. During this period, she trained without any income.

Before the 2020 Asian Race-Walking Championship was cancelled due to the coronavirus pandemic, Jat registered a timing of 1 hour 28 minutes, and 4 seconds in training. That kind of effort would have won her a bronze at Rio 2016.

Regardless of the result in Tokyo, Jat's qualification amidst severe financial ordeals has already made her a national heroine.

Lovlina Borgohain (Boxer)

World No. 4 (69 kg) Lovlina Borgohain's unlikely journey to Tokyo 2020 began in the tiny village of Baro Mukhia, Assam.

Eight years ago, Borgohain was clueless about boxing. She is the daughter of a tea garden worker, and back then money was hard to come by for the Borgohain family.

She said in one of her interviews "I rarely discuss such things because I firmly believe if you want to be successful you don't look back. There was a time when she couldn't afford travel outside her village because bus or train fares were too expensive".

She also said "I remember traveling to the sub-junior nationals in Kolkata, sleeping beside a train compartment toilet with my father. When I look back at those times, I take it as motivation to only get better. Karna hai mujhe (I have to get it done)."

"I'm going to be honest with you, my father couldn't afford boxing attire during that time," she said.

During the first two years of her career across various sub-junior categories, Borgohain travelled to several tournaments without proper boxing attire.

She also mentioned in her interview that "I used to ask other competitors whose bouts were over for their kit. One day a girl insulted me by calling me poor and illiterate because I had requested her attire. I felt insulted, I remember going back home and crying to my father and he consoled me. I would like to thank the Sports Authority of India (SAI) who gave me my first boxing kit, will never forget that day."

She procured her first pair of gloves at the end of 2013; before that, she used to participate in tournaments using regional SAI center or hostel gloves. She had to return these as they were used by several sparring partners during training sessions.

Despite having no early training in boxing, she was selected for the sub-junior state-level camp by the Sports Authority of India (SAI).

During her initial days, she used to do kickboxing, her legs used to lift automatically, resulting in a violation. Hence coaches pushed her hard. Her father convinced her by talking about Shiva Thapa and Mary Kom.

Travel was a big problem as she didn't have enough money for tickets. But slowly she started learning from her coaches, but she didn't get any big results till 2017.

It was in late 2017 that Borgohain's fortunes turned, thanks to the introduction of the 69kg category at the Olympics. Before that, she had been forced to compete in the 75kg category despite being under 70, due to the absence of her desired weight class.

Fighting in the 69kg category, she won a bronze medal at the 2017 Asian Championship in Vietnam. She later registered back-to-back World Championship podium finishes, in 2018 and 2019.

All her initial career struggles finally paid off at the Olympic qualifier in Amman, where she defeated Uzbekistan's Maftunakhon Melieva to secure a ticket to Tokyo. She ultimately won a bronze medal in Tokyo Olympics 2020.

Deepika Kumari (Archery)

A search for food and shelter eventually culminated in the World No. 1 ranking, and that too at just 18 years of age.

Based in the Ratu Chati village of Jharkhand, the Kumari family struggled to earn just Rs. 700 a month - far below the poverty line. With a severe shortage of money and food at home, Deepika took up archery at the Kharsawan training center to reduce the burden on her family.

She practiced with makeshift bamboo bows and used mangoes as targets. But she somehow managed to qualify for the training center's academy project, and in the process obtained free food and lodging.

She took up archery in the beginning because she came to know that the training academy gave free food and stay. Her family was struggling, they ate once a day and felt that she needed to reduce the burden on her family as there were so many mouths to feed. The academy rejected her at first, but she told them to give her three months and she will prove her talent.

Deepika started participating in various sub-junior competitions, where the prize money was Rs. 500. For a family that earned Rs. 700 a month, winning Rs. 500 was almost like doubling the income.

Participating in these tournaments also helped spread the word of her talent to the national coaches. She was eventually spotted by Tata Academy junior team coach Dharmendra and that changed everything.

She began training at the JRD Tata Sports Complex in Jamshedpur. It was almost like a dream come true. She had never stayed in a hostel with toilets specifically for women. She had never seen such facilities. After the first week, she just prayed to God to stay there forever.

This was also the first time Deepika was introduced to recurve bows and arrows, as opposed to the traditional ones made of wood. She slowly acclimatized herself to the new equipment, and success in national junior tournaments led to international participation.

Deepika was the first-ever Indian sub-junior archer to become a senior national champion. The ace archer turned the clock back to when she boarded her first-ever flight.

She mentioned in one of her interviews "I still remember the first time I sat on a plane. I pinched myself, am I sitting on a plane?"

In 2009, she became the Cadet World Champion, signaling the beginning of an unprecedented era for Indian archery.

Deepika also secured one World Cup, six Asian Championship, two World Championship, one Asian Games, and two Commonwealth Games medals over a decade. However, that success did not translate into Olympics glory - neither in London nor in Rio.

The 25-year-old secured a Tokyo Olympics quota for India by winning the Asian qualifier tournament in Bangkok. Regardless of the result in Tokyo, Deepika's rise from abject poverty to international dominance is worthy of a golden page in the history books.

KT Irfan (Race Walking)

Born in the remote village of Kuniyil in Kerala's Malappuram district, KT Irfan was the first Indian athlete to qualify for the Tokyo 2020 Olympics. He registered a fourth-place finish at the 2019 Asian Race-walking Championship in Japan to seal his berth.

The fifth of seven brothers, KT couldn't even afford shoes ahead of the London 2012 Games. But popular Malayalam actor Mohanlal came to the rescue and donated an undisclosed amount for his campaign.

The new shoes and enhanced training helped KT set the men's 20km national record of 1:20.21 at the London Olympics - a record that still stands eight years later.

During his interview, KT acknowledged actor Mohanlal's help and the state government's assistance in his preparations for the Games.

During that time he was a sepoy in the Army. His salary was only Rs 10,000, the cost of the shoes was Rs 7,000, special walking shoes. So there was no way he was going to afford it before the Games. Thanks to both Mohanlal and the state government that he was able to participate with adequate equipment.

Born to a poor family, KT would practice barefoot in his school. His brother played a massive role in helping him further in his athletic career.

His father was a landless laborer, so it was very tough for him to take up the sport in the beginning. One of his brothers got a job in Dubai and he helped him with funds to fulfill his Olympic dream.

With the help of more grants from the Kerala state government, KT has now been able to buy his father a piece of land and a house in his village.

A low point of KT's career was the 2018 Commonwealth Games in Gold Coast, where he along with triple jumper Rakesh Babu were found with multiple needles in their room. As per the CWG's no-needle policy, this was a violation of the code of conduct.

Upon questioning, the duo came up with inconclusive answers, prompting the authorities to send them back home.

He participated in Tokyo Olympics, after missing out on the Rio edition. He won bronze at the Asian Racewalking Championship 2017 held in Japan.

Helluva Koroth Vismaya (Athlete)

The 22-year-old shot into the limelight at the 2018 Asian Games in Jakarta, when she beat the continent's top women's 400m runner Salwa Eid Naser. In the final leg of the 4x400 women's relay, Vismaya emerged quicker than Naser to help India continue its longest-running win streak.

The daughter of a construction laborer, Vismaya had to set her priorities very early in life.

Education has always been her top priority. She comes from a poor family and she needs to focus on uplifting the status of her family. She faced a lot of hardships, in the beginning, so she wanted to focus on studies more than athletics.

Before the 2018 Asian Games, Vismaya had only run-in school and college tournaments. And her college running was mainly a stepping stone towards earning her BSc in Mathematics degree.

That result greatly enhanced Vismaya's status in India and especially in Kerala, where she has now become a household name. But surprisingly, Vismaya considers athletics as nothing but an avenue to complete her education.

An A-grade student, Vismaya began running in class 11 at the age of 17, which was quite late for a future Asian Games gold medalist.

She was spotted by former US Collegiate coach Galina Bukharin, who backed Vismaya for Jakarta despite her poor timings in the qualifiers. The Kannur-based sprinter won an Asian Games gold with just four months of senior practice, an unheard-of feat in the sport.

She participated in the 4x400m mixed relay team and the team consists of Muhammed Anas, VK Vismaya, Jisna Matthew, and Nirmal Noah (Tokyo Olympics 2020). They qualified for Tokyo Olympics 2020 by finishing in the top 8 of the 2019 World Athletics Championship held in Qatar.

O P Jaisha (Athlete)

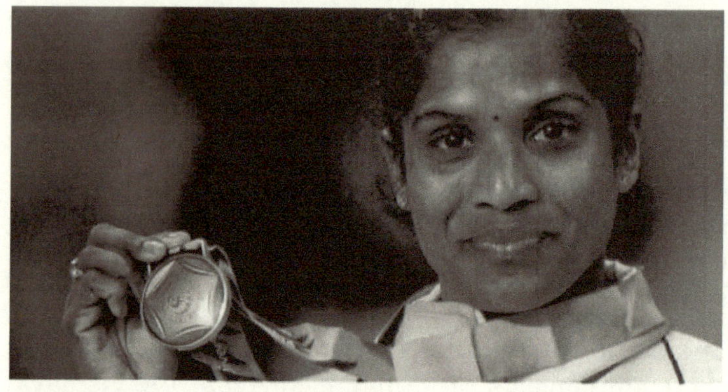

She is another remarkable athlete to represent the nation in the 2016 Rio Olympics. She is the current national record holder in the marathon, a distinction she achieved by clocking 2:34:43 at the 2015 World Championships in Beijing. She is also a former national record holder in the 3000 meters steeplechase.

She comes from a lower-income family in the Waynad district of Kerala, which faced further hardships when her father met with an accident. She was just five when all the responsibility fell upon her and her mother to keep the family sustained.

"When you have nothing to fall back, you must grab the opportunity that comes your way and put your heart and soul into athletics. I did just that at Assumption College," Jaisha says in one of her interviews.

Unavailability of food forced her to survive on mud several times.

As a child, she used to get up at 5 am, milk the cows her mother bought on loan, and then walk a mile to the local milk society to sell the milk and walk back home. Then she would walk another two kilometers to school.

She would run back home during the lunch break to eat and was lucky if she found anything to eat at all. In the evening, she would once again make the two-kilometer return trip to the milk society. This served as Jaisha's high-altitude training while growing up.

As a teenager, Jaisha was adamant about attending a sports-cum-cultural festival 3 km away from her hometown. She annoyed her mother about it till finally, tired of refusing her, Jaisha's mother gave in, saying "Do what you want."

This was the only time Jaisha defied her mother's wishes and set off from Thrissilery, the tribal region in north Kerala's Wayanad district. She went to the festival as a spectator but was persuaded to participate in the 800m race by a local coach struggling to fill in last-minute dropouts from his team.

In her first such race, she was barefoot, competed with the national school games champion, and, to everyone's amazement, went on to win first place; achieving an unbelievable 100-meter lead over the national school champion.

She ran home and proudly showed her family the winning certificate. Her victory brought tears of joy to a mother battling depression, a bed-ridden father, and three elder sisters.

She decided then that she would run to make and break milestones and to lift her family out of the miserable poverty that had befallen them.

At the age of 21, she had a great start, and her career as an athlete looked promising, but instead of scaling greater heights, her performance took a downward turn. Family commitments took her time and energy, leaving her devoid of the two ingredients essential to every athlete's success.

She used the prize money earned at the Doha Asian Games to arrange her sister's marriages, sold her house to pay off an earlier loan, and settle medical bills for her father who was still bed-ridden. Her body too protested strongly with injury and health problems cropping up.

Victories at the national level and a bronze in the 1,500 meters at the Asian Athletics Championships could not offset her below-average performance in other crucial events.

Her situation was made worse by a stress fracture that killed her London Olympics dream. Her career seemed to come to a standstill at 30 and she found herself wanting to quit.

Following her exclusion from the national camp after an unsatisfactory attempt at the Asian championships in Pune, Jaisha and her husband visited the Sports Authority of India's high altitude training center in Dharamshala where Jaisha slowly but steadily regained her form and strength over nine months.

If she had a few years to prepare for the clash of the best Marathoners of the world, she could have given herself a fighting chance.

She has been able to rescue her family from poverty and has repaid the family loans. The fame she brought to her village influenced the Grameen bank to waive off a portion of the loan.

She says, "Today, my family has three square meals; every day... 365 days of the year." As a breadwinner for her impoverished family, she is already a winner.

Achievements:

Year	Competition	Venue	Position	Event	Notes
2005	Asian Indoor Games	Bangkok, Thailand	1st	1500 meters	04:15.7
			1st	3000 meters	09:38.4
2006	Asian Indoor Championships	Pattaya, Thailand	2nd	1500 meters	04:18.5
			3rd	3000 meters	09:26.7
2006	Asian Games	Doha, Qatar	3rd	meters	15:41.9
2014	Asian Games	Incheon, South Korea	3rd	meters	04:13.5
2015	Mumbai Marathon	Mumbai, India	8th	Marathon	2:37:29 NR
	World Championships	Beijing, China	18th	Marathon	2:34:43 NR

Khushbir Kaur (Race Walking)

She is the first Indian woman to win an Asian medal in a 20 km race walking. Kaur hails from Rasalpur Kalan, a village near Amritsar. Her family has roots in the farming community. Her mother Jasbir Kaur encouraged her to take up sports professionally. She lost her father at the age of six and was raised by her mother.

Her mother was forced to take up low-status jobs at the houses of other people to keep the family running. But Khushbir decided she would not give up and her determination finally paid off when she won the 2008 Junior Nationals without even wearing shoes.

The fastest walking Indian girl belonged to one of the most impoverished villages in Punjab and was unaware of the sport till she got into it. She was like any other girl till her father passed away owning to a cardiac arrest.

<u>**Achievements**</u>:

- She participated in the 2013 World Championships in the 20 km walk category. She clocked 1:34:28 and finished 39th.

- At the 2014 Asian walking championships in Japan, she came third with a timing of 1:33:37.

- She won the Arjuna Award after her consecutive victories in International sports events.

- 2016 Rio Olympics, she secured 54th position in 20 km race walk and thus gouged a mark in the prestigious international sports championship. She took 1 hour, 40 minutes, and 30 seconds to complete the distance of the race which was far away from her previous national records.

- 2018 Commonwealth Games, she finished fourth in the women's 20 kilometers racewalk event where she clocked the time of 1 hour, 39 minutes and 21 seconds.

Laishram Sarita Devi (Boxing)

Laishram Sarita Devi is an Indian boxer from Manipur. She is a national champion and a former world champion in the lightweight class.

Sarita Devi was born in Manipur. She used to spend her time helping her parents in collecting firewood and in the fields, which helped her build the stamina she has today.

She completed her high school in Waithou Mapal High School till the eighth standard and then went to Bal Baidya Mandir, Thoubal to complete her matriculation.

She then went to an open school to complete her twelfth standard to cope with her busy boxing schedule.

She turned professional in boxing in 2000, inspired by the achievements of Muhammad Ali.

<u>**Achievements**</u>:

Sl no	Year	Description
1	2001	She represented India at the Asian Boxing Championships in Bangkok and won a silver medal in her weight class.
2	2005	She was offered the post of Sub-Inspector (SI) by the police department of Manipur, for winning a bronze medal in the 3rd World Women Boxing Championship, Russia .
3	2014	Silver medal in Commonwealth Games.
4	2018	She won Silver Medal at Indian Open International Championships, New Delhi, and bagged a Gold Medal at Sr. National Boxing Championships, Rohtak.

<u>**Controversy**</u>:

Devi entered the 2014 Asian Games in Incheon, South Korea, competing in the lightweight category. With a winning margin of 3–0 both in the Round of 16 and Quarterfinals, she entered the semi-finals to face South Korea's Park Ji-Na on 30 September.

After the match, she was handed a 0–3 defeat verdict by the judges of the match, which turned out to be hugely controversial, considering that Devi had knocked Park out in the third round and also a convincing fourth round, before having rained heavy blows on Park throughout the first two rounds.

Following this, the Indian team protested the decision, which was rejected by the AIBA's technical committee.

At the medal awarding ceremony, Devi refused to accept her bronze medal and handed it over to the silver medallist.

However, she accepted the medal later. This was followed by the provisional suspension of her coaches by the AIBA. She was handed a one-year ban by the AIBA.

Shiva Keshavan (Luge)

Shiva Keshavan is a six-time Olympian and the first Indian representative to compete in **luge** at the Winter Olympic Games. He set a new Asian speed record at 134.3 km/h (83.5 mph) after beating the previous record of 131.9 km/h (82.0 mph) and won a gold medal in the 2011 Asian Luge Cup at Nagano in Japan.

Keshavan is the son of an Indian father from Kerala and an Italian mother, who met while backpacking in the Himalayas in the 1970s. His parents run an Italian restaurant in Himachal Pradesh.

Keshavan skied as a child and won the Junior National Ski Championship in 1995 at the age of 14. At the age of 15, he attended a luge camp at his school conducted by world champion Kemmerer.

He was selected as a promising young athlete and went on to become the youngest person to ever officially qualify for the Olympic Games in luge, attending the 1998 Nagano games at the age of 16.

In 2014, Keshavan collaborated with Duncan Kennedy to train for the 2018 PyeongChang Winter Olympics. Duncan acted as Keshavan's coach while leveraging his technical expertise to improve Keshavan's sled.

Keshavan qualified for his sixth and final Olympics in 2018, where he finished 34th out of 40 athletes in the men's singles event.

In 2014 Shiva Keshavan became the founder-president of the Olympians Association of India and is committed to supporting the Olympic movement in India.

Keshavan often speaks in interviews about his struggles to finance his career. Early in his career, he would borrow sleds for his races. After landing in Montreal for the 2002 games, he hitchhiked to Salt Lake City. In 2006, he did not compete for two seasons due to running out of funds.

Keshavan gets most of his money from crowdfunding on the Internet.

In 2002, the Italian luge team offered Keshavan full use of their coaches and training facilities if he competed under the Italian flag, but he did not take the offer, insisting he wanted to continue representing India. "For me, the dream was to get the Olympics to my hometown, and that was the only reason I was doing it. To show that we are also here."

Keshavan spends time promoting the cause of winter sports in India; a grassroots level luge camp was held in India by Keshavan in 2009 for young athletes interested in trying the sport. Ten were selected to form the Junior National Luge team to train in Japan. Since then, around 200 Indian children have attended his training camps, and after retiring from competition Keshavan plans to focus on recruiting new Indian winter athletes.

<u>Achievements</u>:

- Arjuna Award, - 2020 - First Winter Sport athlete to win the award.
- NDTV Outstanding performer of the year award-winner, 2012.
- Asian Luge cup – Gold Medal, 2011 & 2012.
- Asian Luge cup – Silver Medal, 2009.
- Asian Luge cup – Bronze Medal, 2005 & 2008.
- Youngest luge Olympian in history - 1998 Winter Olympics.
- First Indian luger to qualify for the Winter Olympic Games.

Hima Das (Athlete)

Hima Das, nicknamed *Dhing Express*, is an Indian sprinter from the state of Assam. She holds the current Indian national record in 400 meters with a timing of 50.79 s that she clocked at the 2018 Asian Games in Jakarta, Indonesia.

She is the first Indian athlete to win a gold medal in a track event at the IAAF World U20 Championships.

She was appointed as a Deputy Superintendent of Police (DSP) in Assam Police. under the state's Integrated Sport Policy.

She was born at Kandhulimari village, near the town of Dhing in her home state of Assam to Ranjit Das and Joni Das. Her parents are farmers by profession. She was initially interested in playing football. She used to play football with the boys at her JNV school and had always wanted to pursue a career in football. However, she did not see any prospects for herself in the women's football team in India. Later, upon advice from a school physical education teacher at JNV, she changed to sprint running.

<u>**Achievements**</u>:

Sl no	Year	Description
1	2018	Winner of U20 World championship, 400 meters.
2	2018	National record in 400 meters.
3	2018	She, along with M. R. Poovamma, Sarita Gayakwad, and V. K. Vismaya won the women's 4 × 400 meters relay clocking 3:28.72. Also won a silver medal in the 4 × 400 m mixed relay, which was held for the first time at Asian Games.
4	2018	Arjuna Awardee.
5	2019	200m gold in Poznan Grand Prix in Poland, 200m gold at the Kladno Meet in the Czech Republic.
6	2019	400-meter race in Nové Město, Czech Republic.
7	2021	Hima Das enrolled as a civil servant in the post of Deputy Superintendent of Police of Assam Police Service cadre through Assam Public Service Commission without giving the Common Competitive Examination.

Swapna Barman (Heptathlete)

Swapna Barman is an Indian heptathlete. She won the gold medal at the 2018 Asian Games and placed first in the Heptathlon at the 2017 Asian Athletics Championships.

She was born in Ghospara village near Jalpaiguri, West Bengal in 1996 in a poor Rajbongshi family. She is unusual in having six toes on each foot.

Her mother Basana worked on a tea estate and her father, Panchanan Barman, was a rickshaw driver. and is bed-ridden after having suffered a stroke in 2013, making life tricky for his four children.

She found it difficult to find the right food and her unusual feet caused her pain because she could not afford extra wide running shoes. Swapna uses her prize money to look after her family who lives in a house without a concrete wall. In 2016 she won a scholarship of 1,50,000 rupees in recognition of the success she had at athletics.

In 2016, she was supported by the Go-Sports Foundation through the Rahul Dravid Athlete Mentorship Programme.

Barman won the gold at the 2018 Asian Games, she accomplished this despite a jaw injury. She collapsed during the final event of the 2017 Asian Athletics Championships – Women's heptathlon which was 800 meters. However, Barman had broken many of her records and she had already gained enough points from the previous six events and she had finished fourth in the 800 meters.

In 2020 she lost out on a funding list but said that she would continue to train at her home in Jalpaiguri, West Bengal.

Achievements:

Asian Athletics Championships:

Year	Venue	Event	Points	Result
2017	Kalinga Stadium, Bhubaneswar	Heptathlon	5942	Gold
2019	Khalifa International Stadium, Doha	Heptathlon	5993	Silver

Federation cup:

Year	Venue	Event	Points	Result
2017	JLN Stadium, New Delhi	Heptathlon	5897	Gold

Asian Games:

Year	Venue	Event	Points	Result
2014	Incheon Asiad Main Stadium	Heptathlon	5178	5th place
2018	Gelora Bung Karno Stadium	Heptathlon	6026	Gold

Arpinder Singh (Athlete)

Arpinder has won 14 national gold medals while playing for Punjab. When he won the bronze in CWG in 2014, he hoped to get a DSP post or a Category A job. Haryana offered a higher cash reward to participating players and here in Punjab, he got Rs 6 lakh.

As a retired havildar from Army, his father gets a pension of Rs 12,000. Parents mortgaged gold jewellery for his training. When he chose to play for Haryana, it was heart-breaking for us.

"It was a different feeling when he played for the state where he was born and won medals, getting reward and recognition," Arpinder's 63-year-old father Jagbir Singh told in one of his interviews.

Achievements:

- In June 2014, Singh beat his previous best of 16.84 meters by jumping 17.17 meters at National Inter-State Championships in Lucknow.

- Also he beat the national record previously held by Renjith Maheshwary and also secured qualification for the 2014 Commonwealth Games where he won the bronze medal.

- On August 29, 2018, which is celebrated as National Sports Day in India he won the gold medal in the triple jump event in the 18th Asian games.

- He bagged a bronze medal in the 2014 commonwealth games.

- He also bagged a gold medal in Asian Indoor and Martial arts games.

Dharun Ayyasamy (Athlete)

Dharun was born in a village called Ravuthampalayam near Avinashi in Tiruppur district. When he was in fourth grade, his father died of tuberculosis. Dharun's mother is a school teacher while his sister Sathya plays volleyball for Tamil Nadu. His mother earns Rs 14,000 per month as a teacher, has been doing everything possible to help Dharun succeed in his field of choice.

Dharun completed his schooling at The Century Foundation School in Tirupur where he was coached by Mr. Alagesan and he never looked back since then.

He won silver in men's 400m hurdles, hoping that his silver medal will provide him some recognition and financial support so that he can support his stoic mother, who single-handedly took care of him after his father's death.

Achievements:

- He won 400 meters hurdle gold at the 2016 South Asian Games in Guwahati with a time of 50.54 seconds, finishing 0.03 seconds ahead of fellow Indian Jithin Paul whom he overtook at the last hurdle.

- In July 2016, Dharun was part of the relay team that broke the national 4 × 400 meters relay record at Bangalore and qualified for the Olympics. The quartet of Dharun, Mohammad Anas, Kunhu Muhammed, and Arokia Rajiv clocked 3:00:91, rewriting the national record of 3:02.17 set by themselves four weeks earlier in Turkey. The performance helped the relay team jump to 13th place in the world rankings. It was the third time a men's relay team from India qualified for the Olympics, after 1964 and 2000.

- He won the gold medal in 400 meters hurdle in the 2016 South Asian Games, Guwahati.

- In August 2018, Dharun won the 400-meter hurdles silver medal at the Asian Games in Jakarta with a timing of 48.96 seconds setting a new national record.

Sudha Singh (Athlete)

Sudha Singh is an Indian Olympic athlete in the 3000 meters steeplechase event. A national record holder in the event, she has represented India at international events since 2005. Singh is an Asian Champion in the discipline and has won two gold and four silver medals at varying editions of the Asian Games and the continental championships.

Career highlights:

Sl no	Year	Description
1	2010	2010 Asian Games in Guangzhou, where she won the gold medal in the steeplechase with a time of 9:55.67.
2	2012	Qualified for Olympic Games 2012 after she broke her own 3,000m steeplechase national record with a timing of 9:47.70 secs.
3	2012	Arjuna Awardee.

4	2014	Asian Games held in Incheon, South Korea, Sudha finished fourth, one place behind Lalita Babar who not only won the bronze medal in the 3000m steeplechase event but also broke Sudha's national record, clocking 9:35.37 in the process. However, the gold medallist Ruth Jebet from Bahrain was disqualified on account of stepping inside the track before crossing the line, and Singh was promoted and won the bronze medal.
5	2017	Won gold at Asian Athletic Championship in Bhubaneswar, 3000 meters steeplechase.
6	2018	Won silver in Asian Games, Jakarta, 3000 meters steeplechase.
7	2021	Padma Shri.

Rani Rampal (Hockey)

Rani Rampal was the youngest player in the national team who played at the age of 15 in the 2010 World Cup. She belonged to a poor and very humble family. Her father pulled carts, and his earnings may be Rs 100 per day, and her mother worked as a house help. She got inspired from seeing the players playing hockey. She used to play with a broken hockey stick as she couldn't afford a stick. After playing in this Tokyo Olympic, she is being congratulated by everyone.

During an interview with The Better India, she said,

"*I* grew up in a place where young women and girls were restricted to the four walls of their home. So, when I expressed my wish to play hockey, neither my parents nor my relatives supported me. My parents come from a humble background and weren't very educated. They did not think sports could be a career path, not for girls at least. Besides, my relatives would often tell my father, 'What will she do playing hockey? She will run around the field wearing a short skirt and bring a bad name to your family'."

<u>Career highlights</u>:

- Lead the Indian hockey team in Olympic 2020.

- She was nominated for the ' young woman player of the year award in 2010. She has also been included on the All-Star team of the Asian Hockey Federation based on her performance in the 2010 Asian Games at Guangzhou.

- She was conferred the "Best Young Player of the Tournament" award at the Women's Hockey World Cup 2010.

- She has also adjudged the 'Player of the Tournament' at the 2013 Junior World Cup which India finished with a bronze medal.

- She has been named for the FICCI Comeback of the Year Award 2014.

- She led the Indian women's hockey team as captain in the 2018 Asian Games, where they won a silver medal and was India's flag-bearer for the closing ceremony of the games.

- Major Dhyan Chand Khel Ratna (2020) - Highest Sporting Honour of India.

- Padma Shri (2020).

Vandana Katariya (Hockey)

Vandana Katariya was born in Roshnabad, Uttarakhand. Her father, Nahar Singh, worked as a Master Technician in Bhel, Haridwar, who passed away just before the Tokyo Olympics.

Vandana is the first Indian woman who scored a hat-trick at the Olympics.

Her family was subjected to casteist slurs after India lost to Argentina in the semifinals. Certain upper-caste men hurled abuses at Katariya's family saying that the team lost the Olympic semifinal as it had too many Dalit players.

In an interview, she called the bronze medal her favorite moment, "It has to be when we won the bronze medal at the World Cup in Germany. My father was called by the media and he had tears in his eyes. So, making my father proud is the best moment of my hockey career."

<u>Career highlights</u>:

- Katariya was picked in the Indian junior team in 2006 and she made it to the senior national team in 2010.

- She was a part of the team that won bronze at the 2013 Junior World Cup in Mönchengladbach, Germany. She was India's top scorer in the tournament, having scored 5 goals in 4 games.

- She won her 100th cap while playing against Canada in the 2014 Commonwealth Games in Glasgow, Scotland.

- She is quick, can score goals, can defend, and is improving all the time," the Indian women's hockey team's stop-gap coach Roelant Oltmans said after her performance in Round 2 League.

- In November 2016, Katariya was retained as the skipper of the Indian women's hockey team for the Test Series against Australia and led the team in Melbourne from 23 to 30 November.

- The Indian team won a silver at the Asian Champion Trophy, in 2018, losing to Korea. Vandana Katariya won the player of the tournament award.

- In the 2020 Summer Olympics in Tokyo, Vandana became the first Indian woman to score an Olympic hat-trick in hockey.

- On August 8, 2021, she was appointed the brand ambassador of the Centre's 'Beti Bachao, Beti Padhao Andolan'.

Virender Singh Yadav (Deaf Wrestler)

Virender Singh Yadav is an Indian freestyle wrestler. Virender Singh was born to a farmers' family of Sasroli village, near Jhajjar in Haryana. His father, Ajit Singh, was a CISF *Jawan*, while his mother, Manna Devi, is a homemaker.

Virender was inspired to take up wrestling by his father and uncle, who were wrestlers as this was a family tradition passed on by generations. Virender, as a deaf kid, was bullied in the village and his uncle Surinder Pehelwan brought him to Delhi to live at the CISF *akhara* with him and his father.

Watching his father and uncle wrestle, Virender developed an interest in wrestling and they also found talent in him and started honing his skills. Kumar trained in pehlwani wrestling at Chhatrasal Stadium and Guru Hanuman *akhara.*

Virender's first success came at the National Rounds of the World Cadet Wrestling Championships in 2002, where he won the gold medal. Even though the win meant automatic qualification for the world event, he was unfairly disqualified from going to the world event by the Wrestling Federation of India (WFI), citing his deafness as the reason for doing so. It has to be said here that the world body doesn't disqualify deaf players or disabled players from the event but the WFI sent the Silver medallist and Virender was ignored. This was his initiation into the world of discrimination which dogged him throughout his career.

After this, in the year 2005, he got to know of the Deaflympics, formerly The World Games for the Deaf or The Silent Games, and keen on showing his mettle made it to the 2005 Summer Deaflympics in Melbourne, Australia, and won the gold medal.

He never gave up on the dream of representing India at the Olympics, but consistent discrimination and lack of knowledge on the part of the Wrestling Federation of India meant that he could never get referees that could govern matches for the deaf.

He focused on the deaf games and went on winning medals at the international level.

<u>**Career highlights**</u>:

- Competing in the 74 kg weight division, he has won 3 Deaflympics Gold Medals and a bronze medal in 4 appearances.

- He won gold medals at the 2005 Summer Deaflympics (Melbourne, Australia), 2013 Summer

Deaflympics (Sofia, Bulgaria), and 2017 Summer Deaflympics (Samsun, Turkey).

- He also won a bronze at the 2009 Summer Deaflympics (Taipei, Chinese Taipei).

- Virender also won the world title at the world championship and has gold, silver, and bronze medals at the three World Deaf Wrestling Championships that he has been to.

- Virender won gold at the 2016 World Deaf Wrestling Championship (Tehran, Iran), silver at the 2008 World Deaf Wrestling Championship (Yerevan, Armenia), and a bronze at the 2012 World Deaf Wrestling Championship (Sofia, Bulgaria).

- In July 2015, he received the prestigious Arjuna Award.

- Kumar is presently employed with the Sports Authority of India as a Junior Sports Coach training the next generation of wrestlers.

Virender Singh also became the subject of a documentary titled, Google Pehelwan. The name of the film translates to 'The Mute Wrestler', which although is a politically incorrect term was used because that is how the world knew him and his real name was almost forgotten in the wrestling circles, and even his family usually referred to him as Google. The 45-minute documentary film went on to play at film festivals across the Globe and also won the highest Indian film honor, National Film Award in the year 2015.

Dingko Singh (Boxer)

Dingko Singh was an Indian boxer who won the gold medal at the 1998 Asian Games in Bangkok. He was born in a remote village called Sekta in the Imphal East District, Manipur to a very poor family. Dingko had to fight back adversities from the beginning of his life and was brought up in an orphanage.

He is considered to have been one of the most outstanding boxers India ever produced. He won the King's Cup in Bangkok in 1997 and won the Asian Games gold in the 1998 Bangkok Games.

He was service personnel of the Indian Navy.

The trainers at a Special Area Games Scheme initiated by the Sports Authority of India identified the hidden talents of Dingko during the assessment camp from Dec. 1990 to Jan. 1991 at Khuman Lampak, Imphal.

He was inducted at SAI SAG Khuman Lampak, Imphal w.e.f. 12 Feb. 1991 and trained under the guidance of Boxing coach Shri. Leishangthem Ibomcha Singh. In the same year, in his debut at the National level championship, he won the gold medal. This achievement brought Dingko into the eyes of the selectors and coaches, who began to see him as a promising boxing star of India.

<u>Career highlights</u>:

- He made his debut in the arena of international boxing in 1997 and won the King's Cup 1997 held in Bangkok, Thailand.

- He also represented India at the 1998 Asian Games and the 2000 Summer Olympics.

- He was selected for the Indian boxing squad which participated at the Asian Games in Bangkok in 1998.

- To commemorate his excellence in the sport of boxing, and his extraordinary contribution to the nation by his consistent efforts and dedication, Dingko Singh was honored with the Arjuna Award in 1998 and later with the Padma Shri Award, the country's fourth-highest civilian award, in 2013.

For unknown reasons, he was dropped from the team at the last minute and dejected Dingko went on a drinking spree, collapsing after a long session of drinks. Eventually, he was selected and the event proved to be the pinnacle of his career as he created history by winning the gold medal in the 54 kg Bantamweight category.

He died, on Thursday 10 June 2021, after a long battle with liver cancer. He had been fighting the disease since 2017.

A movie inspired by his life is expected to be released by 2022.

Your take away from the stories:

Dream big and aim big. Whatever be the situation, your target should be always your goal. People will say many things like " Ye Karke Kya Hoga" just ignore them.

Nowadays people feel jealous if you do some extraordinary things, then they try to find out the loopholes and they also try to demotivate.

Those who fall under their trap, won't touch the finishing line of the goal. It's not about sports, depending upon your interest, set your target, go for it. I always say, define the process, trust the process.

There are no shortcuts, you have to take lots of pain but once you achieve your goal, only you can feel the sacrifices you have done during the process.

Pain is temporary, pride is permanent. You may fail 100 times during the process but never feel like " Ye Humse Nehi Hoga". Patience is the key, stay focussed.